© Copyright 2021 - All rights reserved.

You may not reproduce, duplicate or send the contents of this book without direct written permission from the author. You cannot here despite any circumstances blame the publisher or hold him or her to legal responsibility for any reparation, compensations, or monetary forfeiture owing to the information included herein, either in a direct or an indirect way.

Legal Notice: This book has copyright protection. You can use the book for personal purposes. You should not sell, use, alter, distribute, quote, take excerpts, or paraphrase in part or whole the material contained in this book without obtaining the permission of the author first.

Disclaimer Notice: You must take note that the information in this document is for casual reading and entertainment purposes only.

We have made every attempt to provide accurate, up-to-date, and reliable information. We do not express or imply guarantees of any kind. The person who read admits that the writer is not occupied in giving legal, financial, medical, or other advice. We put this book content by sourcing various places.

Please consult a licensed professional before you try any techniques shown in this book. By going through this document, the book lover comes to an agreement that under no situation is the author accountable for any forfeiture, direct or indirect, which they may incur because of the use of material contained in this document, including, but not limited to, — errors, omissions, or inaccuracies.

Thank you for purchasing this coloring book!
I appreciate your purchase! I am very excited to share it with you.
I hope that you enjoy this product as much as we have. If you do, please consider writing a positive review on Amazon, which can be very helpful to support our artistic work and the publication of other books for you!
If you have any questions, please email me at:
monicagopublish20@yahoo.com